THE BODY COACH™

Firmer Thighs & Trimmer Waist

Paul Collins

HINKLER BOOKS

Creative Director: Sam Grimmer

Editor: Tom Doig

Design: Katherine Power

Photography: Ned Meldrum

First published in 2004
by Hinkler Books Pty Ltd
17-23 Redwood Drive
Dingley Victoria 3172 Australia
www.hinklerbooks.com

Printed and bound in China

HINKLER
BOOKS

ISBN 1 7412 1797 0

CONTENTS

NOTE: 20-30-40 Exercise Principle™, 3B's Principle™, Collins-Technique™ and 2-Day Meal Rotation™ are trademarks of Paul Collins The Body Coach®. The 3 Hour Rule® is a registered trademark of Paul Collins.

INTRODUCTION

Hi! Welcome to *The Body Coach: Firmer Thighs and Trimmer Waist*. I'm Paul Collins, your exclusive Personal Trainer, and I'm here to guide you through a unique lower body workout focused on trimming your waist and firming the muscles of the hips, buttocks and thighs.

Whatever your age, body shape or level of fitness, this program will provide you with the necessary tools to help you achieve your goals. All you have to do is follow the step-by-step guidelines I'll prescribe for each exercise and you will learn how to use your muscles effectively, firming them up and improving your overall body shape. You'll also improve your posture, balance, coordination, physical strength and flexibility, all of which can help slow down the ageing process.

As your hip and thigh muscles respond to exercise and become stronger, they'll start to shape, trim and tone up having a dramatic effect on the overall shape of your body. What I want is for you to develop the best body you can. Take a moment. Close your eyes and picture in your mind what you want to look and feel like, then use this picture every day as a motivation in working towards your goal of firmer thighs and a trimmer waist. Remember, it's never too late to begin exercising, to make a positive improvement to your body shape and your health.

Before we get started I will teach you a few important exercise principles to ensure you maintain good body posture and can maximise your muscle toning potential—focusing on those finer details of each movement that make all the difference. My revolutionary 20-30-40 Exercise Principle™ will help guide you through a beginner, intermediate and advanced level over the coming weeks. If you apply yourself to this program and practice regularly, some of the benefits you can expect include:

- More shapely legs
- Firmer buttocks and thighs
- Trimmer waist
- Increased control and strength
- Improved bone density
- Greater flexibility
- Increased confidence
- Better posture
- More energy.

Remember, energy creates energy, so just by starting this program you are taking a step towards better health. As your personal coach, I'm here to guide and motivate you. I look forward to working with you!

Paul Collins

Award Winning Personal Trainer

PRACTICAL MATTERS

CURRENT HEALTH

It is recommended you gain clearance from your doctor before performing these exercises, particularly if you have had any previous injuries to these areas (namely lower back, stomach, hip, knee or ankle) or if you are pregnant. Your doctor may then advise you on which exercises are suitable.

EQUIPMENT

The Body Coach: Firmer Thighs and Trimmer Waist requires no special equipment. All you need is an exercise mat, a clear space and few household items, such as a towel and a solid, stable chair. A clear space and non-slip surface should be made available to perform these exercises. An exercise mat or towel can be used on a flat surface for support. Exercise is best practised wearing tight-fitting sports clothing. Follow each movement step by step. You will need to listen to your body and recognise its warning signs, taking care to not strain your muscles or joints. If you should feel any sudden pain or dizziness whilst exercising, stop immediately. If necessary, seek appropriate medical advice before continuing.

WARMING UP AND COOLING DOWN

Warming up the muscles plays an important role in preparing the body mentally and physically for the exercises ahead. A warm shower and stretch followed by light movement (such as walking) will help warm and increase blood flow to the muscles. This also ensures a good range of movement is possible, without tension or stiffness. After exercising, light movement and stretching help to reduce muscle soreness the following day.

HYDRATION

Drink a glass of water (250ml) 15 minutes before exercising. Keep a water bottle by your side and take small sips throughout these workouts. When you finish exercising, drink another glass of water plus a further eight glasses spread throughout the day.

3Bs PRINCIPLE™

Before you get started, there are a number of practical matters to consider. The muscles of the lower body, along with the waistline (abdominal and lower back) are instrumental in helping you maintain good posture. Applying correct technique from the onset will help support the spine, improve your posture and strengthen your legs, abdomen and other targeted muscle groups. My experience as a personal trainer has taught me that maintaining good technique and posture whilst exercising will achieve greater long-term results. To help achieve this, you should follow the 3Bs Principle™ when exercising:

1. Brace – neutral spine and abdominal bracing.

2. Breath – maintain deep breathing pattern.

3. Body Position – maintain good form.

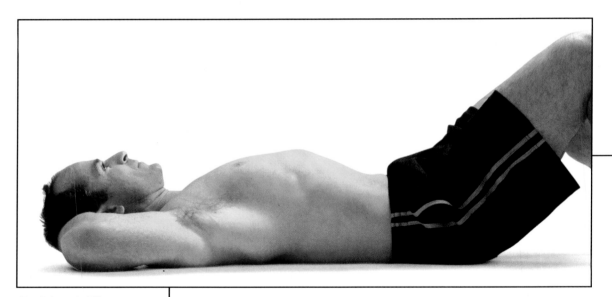

Position 1. Tilt your pelvis backwards, flattening your lower back into the floor.

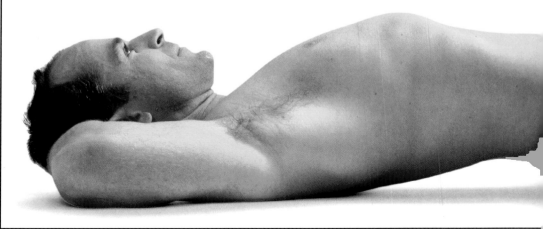

Position 2. Tilt your pelvis in the opposite direction, creating an arch under your lower bac

BRACE
NEUTRAL SPINE

Learning how to control the movement and position of the spine prevents stress and imbalances. The aim is to develop a better awareness of your body position by practicing the neutral spine position—whether sitting, kneeling, lying or standing.

As you begin to move your spine and pelvis through a range of motion you will find a mid-point, which activates the muscles that support the spine and makes you feel elongated and comfortable. As a result, the stress placed on the spine, especially the lower back and neck, will be reduced. In many instances, people may find their bodies have developed stress points through the mid-back and buttock regions—another important reason to consult a physiotherapist and doctor before starting.

The importance of neutral spine cannot be emphasised enough, as it allows your spine to elongate and relax. Before starting an exercise it can be helpful to gently roll the lower back between the start and end positions and then fall comfortably between the two.
The following photograph promotes neutral spine in a lying position on one's back.

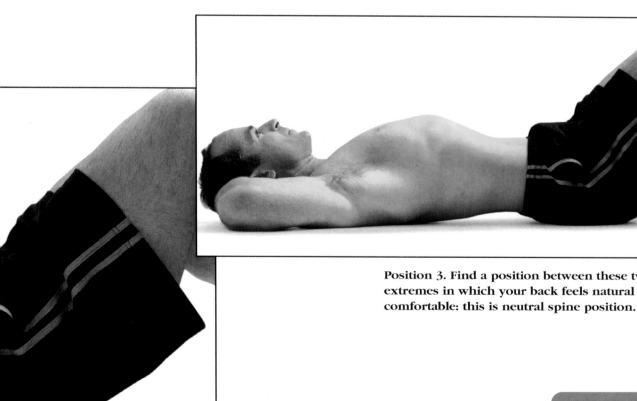

Position 3. Find a position between these two extremes in which your back feels natural and comfortable: this is neutral spine position.

NOTE: Unless otherwise stated, you should always work from position 3 throughout these exercises.

ABDOMINAL BRACING

Abdominal bracing plays an important role in trimming your waistline. Combining neutral spine and deep breathing with abdominal bracing teaches you to contract your abdominal (stomach) muscles. These muscles play an important role in developing an awareness of your body's movement in space and time, and control over the quality of that movement. Abdominal bracing and breathing combinations will be referred to throughout this book as a reference point for most exercise, for example, firstly brace and breathe, then adapt exercise position to accompany these movements.

Initially, breathing may feel short and the stomach might be hard to hold in, but with practice you will improve your ability to contract your stomach muscles, protect your lower back and breathe more efficiently, without tensing other muscles of the body. Over time you will become more efficient with breathing and will be able to relax—yet control—the contraction of the surrounding muscles for better posture and muscle toning.

NOTE: In a standing position, maintaining a neutral spine position (natural curve of the spine), take a deep breath inwards through your nose, then as you breathe out through your mouth, draw your navel (belly button) inwards towards your spine. Continue breathing in through your nose and out through your mouth deeply, whilst holding your stomach in and exercising. As we introduce movement of the arms and legs into the equation through exercise we challenge the abdominal brace position.

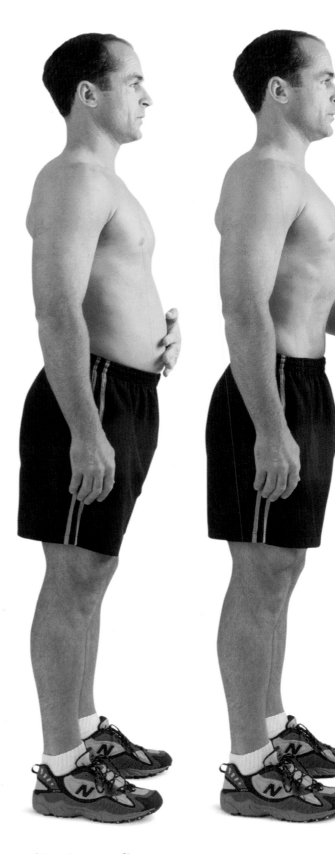

Abdominal Bracing: standing.

BREATHING

Throughout normal everyday activities, the nervous system usually controls our respirations automatically, meeting the body's demands without our conscious concern. When we are passive or resting, our demands for oxygen are small and our breathing is slow and shallow. When there is an increased demand for oxygen, breathing becomes much deeper and swifter. When you exercise, more carbon dioxide from the muscles is pushed into your blood. This triggers a signal in your brain to make you breathe faster and deeper so that you supply more oxygen to your working muscles.

The whole purpose of our respiratory systems is to get oxygen from the air around us into the blood, and then expel waste carbon dioxide from the blood out into the atmosphere. Whilst performing each exercise, the aim is to control the rhythm of our oxygen supply by being conscious of our breathing patterns.

In most cases, breathing controls the pace and speed of each exercise movement. The easiest way to remember when to breathe in and breathe out is: breathe out when you exert a force, and breathe in with recovery. For example: breathe in as you lower the body in a squat, and breathe out as you return up to a standing position. In general, breathe in for one second and breathe out for one second. This pace can be modified to suit each exercise.

NOTE: To maximise your training results, breathe in deeply through the nose, then forcefully out through the mouth with pursed lips (like blowing up a balloon or blowing out candles) for a count of two with each exercise, unless otherwise advised.

Breathe deep into lungs.

Blow out through pursed lips.

BODY POSITION

Good body position and correct movement patterns are important because they provide an indication of the quality of movement being performed, and let you know when to stop. By combining all 3Bs—bracing, breathing and maintaining a good body position—you are in control of the movement pattern being performed. As muscle fatigue sets in, whether after five seconds or 40 seconds, the 3Bs are being jeopardised and you should stop the exercise. Loss of form or feelings of pain are indications that your are overdoing it, which can lead to injury. To avoid this, always maintain good body position, bracing and breathing as a guideline. Work at a comfortable pace, well within your limits, practising these exercises regularly over the coming weeks and months. This way, strength and toning will occur naturally. Don't try to achieve everything overnight. If you are patient and persistent, you will be rewarded.

Adapting the poise of a ballet dancer with each exercise is a great example of what is required whilst exercising. Your commitment to the exercises at hand also requires focus for a short period of time that imitates preparing for the start of a running or swimming race. This poise and focus ensures correct body position throughout the movement that maximises your exercise results. These improvements will also help to develop strength and confidence in other areas of your life.

COLLINS-TECHNIQUE™

The squat exercise is important because it is the mainstay of everyday activity and daily movement patterns, for example: bending, lifting, carrying, lowering, raising, sitting and standing. More importantly, a good squat pattern may reduce the risk of lower back pain, which research shows may affect eight out of every 10 people. As a result I have developed the Collins-Technique™ Squat Pattern, which in 60 seconds will help you to maximise the use of the muscles that tone and shape your buttocks and legs.

To effectively work the muscles of the legs and buttocks, a person must activate the appropriate muscles involved in the movement pattern and avoid emphasis on others. This may entail reprogramming the movement pattern of a number of joints. A person's squat range depends on ankle, knee and hip flexibility and awareness of one's centre of gravity. Learning the proper mechanics can make all the difference in toning and reshaping your legs and avoiding lower back pain.

SELF-TESTING

If you stand in front of a mirror or have someone assess your squat mechanics whilst lowering the body, what do you see?

- Do your heels rise off the ground as you lower?
- Does one knee (or both knees) drop in as you lower?
- Does one foot (or both feet) roll inwards?
- Do you lose your balance—falling forwards or backwards?
- Do your legs reach a 90-degree angle?
- Are you knees in front of your toes?
- Do your hips drop or twist?

These are some common faults.

Poor form.

FOOT AWARENESS

To develop a good squat pattern, the foot position as well as the arch of the foot is crucial. Concentrate on distributing your weight on the footprint of the sole of your foot, without lifting or rolling the foot. Next is rolling the knees out to realign your leg and develop muscle control for maintaining a natural foot arch. This approach is used in all standing exercises.

Adopting a good squat position will help realign your body and maximise muscle functioning. In most cases this translates to acquiring the correct body position for toning and reshaping the muscles of your lower body. The reason why many people have been unsuccessful in the past is due to incorrect movement patterns. With all exercises performed on your feet, this approach should be used.

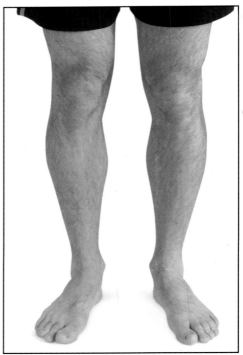

Poor alignment: ankles rolled inwards.

NOTE: Flat feet or rolled-in feet and knees place tremendous stress the joints of the ankle, knee and h areas. In some cas this leads to shin soreness whilst walking and tensi in the lower back.

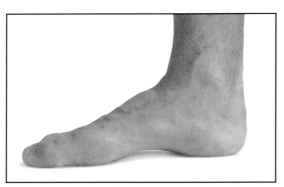

Poor foot awareness: flat foot and weak ankle.

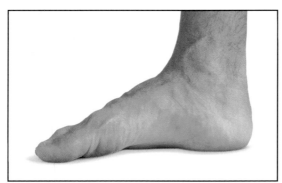

Good foot awareness: holding and developing a foot arch.

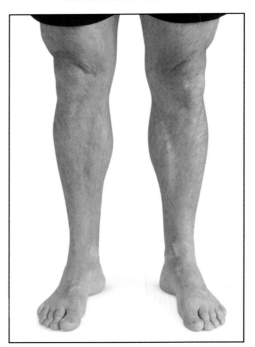

Good alignment: nees rolled out and weight distributed on footprint, leading to a healthy (natural) foot arch. This maximises the use of leg and buttock muscles for toning and reshaping.

ONE LEG BALANCE

In order to develop the natural arch of the foot for correct alignment and core-strength, we need the weight equally balanced on the footprint. To achieve this, extend your arms out to the side, parallel to the ground. Then lift your left leg off the ground, bringing the sole of your left foot to rest on the inside of the leg of your right knee. In doing this, notice the corrections the balancing foot and leg make in holding a foot arch.

Repeat balance on opposite leg.

DEVELOPING A GOOD SQUAT PATTERN

Turn sideways into doorframe (or pole) and grip with hands for support. Stand close and keep your weight even and centred. The aim is to slide the hands down the doorframe (or pole) as you simultaneously bend at the hips, knees and ankles. In many cases, it may feel as though you are falling backwards until your body's timing improves. Hence, sit back with your buttock region as though you are sitting down, but with the goal of keeping the upper body forward for maintaining a good centre of gravity—shoulders over knees over feet. Initially you will feel your weight go backwards, which may feel uncomfortable at first. This is the reason why we are holding the wall or pole for support as we lower. Keeping the knees aligned over the toes at all times, with the hips, knees and ankles working together, you will find the angle of the body lined up from the shoulders, knees and toes. As you develop confidence, the aim is to reduce the pressure of your hands on the wall or pole, and then perform the exercise without any support. This further develops good body position, maximising muscle toning and fat burning.

Adapting the natural foot arch position on both feet as used in the one-leg balance, maintain the weight on your footprint with your knees aligned over your toes. Simultaneously bend at the hips, knees and ankles, taking your buttocks backwards as you lower and maintain the pressure on a healthy footprint. In a short period of time, you will improve your muscle and body awareness and be able to perform the movement with less support from your hands, eventually with none.

Many people find using a solid chair a great transition tool for support and balance while perfecting the movement pattern. Think of it as like having skiing or golf lessons to get the movements right—practice makes perfect! You'll continue to improve the more you practice these movement patterns, which form the basis of all lower body exercises.

NOTE: Simultaneously bend at the hip, knees and ankles to balance body weight keeping it even.

Start

Mid-point

20-30-40 EXERCISE PRINCIPLE™

Whatever your current fitness level or ability you'll find a truly effective program with the introduction of the 20-30-40 Exercise Principle™. Here, I have devised a three-step workout plan to accommodate the beginner, intermediate and advanced exerciser. If you are just starting out or returning to exercise, working out for up to 20 seconds an exercise is a good starting point. Those who consider themselves as having a good fitness base or intermediate fitness level can exercise for up to 30 seconds, whilst the more advanced exerciser can work out for up to 40 seconds each exercise—putting the 20-30-40 Exercise Principle™ into action.

Always start off slowly and work well within your limits. Using 20 seconds as your starting point, work up to 20 seconds per exercise, stopping at any time prior. At times your keenness to participate may will you to work past this point. However, my suggestion is to take it slowly, building up to 20 seconds with each exercise for a month to allow your body to adjust. The exercises prescribed in this book are safe and highly effective in toning and shaping your body; but care must be taken in the first few weeks to avoid overdoing it and enduring any delayed onset muscle soreness (DOMS effect) that often follows any new movement pattern. That's why my chief focus is on maintaining proper form and technique with the 3Bs Principle™, whilst working within your own limits.

Have patience. It is your consistency and regular participation in these exercises, combined with a healthy eating plan and more incidental movement throughout the day, that will see you improve your overall fitness and appearance. As your body and its muscles adapt, you can progressively increase the intensity of your exercise by working through the 20-30-40 Exercise Principle™.

GETTING TO KNOW YOUR BODY

Knowing your muscles is vitally important in making sure you are exercising the right ones. If an exercise targets a specific muscle group and you place stress on a different group, you will not achieve the results you desire. It is therefore important to follow the finer details of each exercise, as I will prescribe. It is the finer details of a movement that make all the difference in reaching your goals. It is also important to regularly practise the personal training principles as previously prescribed in order to ensure correct movement patterns for maximising your muscle-toning potential.

1 Lower Back: muscles that support the spine and pelvis.

2 Gluteal (Buttocks): muscles that contribute to hip movement and pelvic stability.

3 Hamstrings: muscles of the back of the thigh that flex the knee.

4 Thigh (Quads): muscles that extend the knee.

5 Waist (Abdominals): flexion of trunk and compresses abdomen.

6 Obliques: flexion, rotation and compression of abdomen.

7 Hip (Pelvis): attachment of muscles of the spine, leg and abdomen.

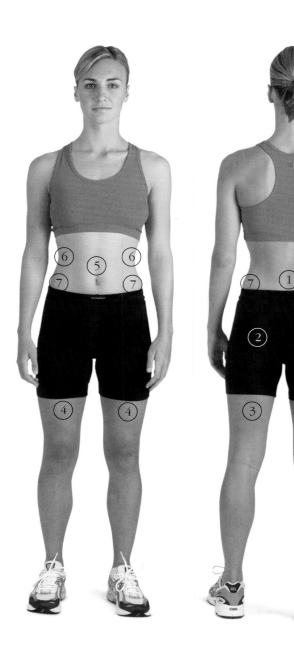

PILATES PRINCIPLES LEG AND WAIST WORKOUT

4 POINT KNEELING SEQUENCE

WARM-UP 1: ABDOMINAL BRACING AND BREATHING

Target area: activates abdominal and breathing muscles to improve body awareness and muscle control for exercises that follow.

1 Kneel on the floor with your hands directly under your shoulders and knees below your hip region.

2 Find neutral spine position (natural curve of the spine), keeping your head level and shoulders high.

3 Take a deep breath inwards through your nose, then as you breathe out through your mouth, draw your belly in towards your spine and hold without changing your neutral spine position.

4 Focus on holding this abdominal brace and neutral spine position for a minimum of five deep breaths. Repeat if necessary.

These positions create a strong base for other exercises that follow.

WARM-UP 2: SWIMMING

Target area: *works the hip, buttock and thigh region, strengthens the lower back and balances the pelvic and shoulder region.*

Start

Mid-point

1 Kneel on knees and hands and create an equilibrium between all four points.

2 Breathing in through the nose, then out through the mouth with pursed lips, draw your belly in towards the spine and hold.

3 Maintaining a strong abdominal brace and neutral spine position, forcefully breathe out through pursed lips whilst simultaneously extending your leg backwards with knee slightly flexed, opposite arm pointing forward.

4 Resisting any arching of the lower back or neck, breathe in and bring leg and arm back to starting position, without relaxing muscles.

5 Repeat on opposite side, maintaining tension on muscles at all times.

THE SIDE-KICK SERIES

LATERAL LEG LIFTS

Target area: *works the inner and outer thigh, strengthens buttocks and balances pelvic region.*

1 Lie on side of body, with lower arm resting under head and upper arm forward supporting the weight of the body.

2 Breathing in through the nose, then out through the mouth with pursed lips, draw your belly in and brace your abdominal muscles, maintaining a neutral spine.

3 Breathing in, tighten thigh.

4 Breathing out, slowly raise your upper leg to 45 degrees, without twisting the leg, and keeping the foot turned down—keeping the heel the high point.

5 Breathe in and lower the leg in a controlled motion.

INS AND OUTS

Target area: *works the thigh, strengthens the buttocks and balances pelvic region.*

NOTE: Repeat Lateral Leg Lifts and Ins and Outs with other leg after shoulder bridge exercise.

1 Having just completed the lateral leg lifts, stay in the same position.
2 Breathing in, bring the knee of the upper leg into the chest.
3 Breathing out, extend the upper leg out in line with lower leg keeping the heel the high point, approximately 30cm off the ground.

THE HUNDRED DRILL

Target area: *works the abdominal muscles, strengthens breathing and balances stomach and neck muscles.*

1 Lie on your back, knees bent and arms by your side.

2 Breathing out, curl upper body and raise legs vertically. Hold your arms parallel to ground—palms facing downwards.

3 Keeping shoulders raised off the ground and abdominals braced, pulse your arms up and down through a 30cm range.

4 Inhale through your nose and breathe out through your mouth as you continue to pulse arms.

Beginner

NOTE: Work up to 20 seconds in this position to start with and build your strength from here. To challenge yourself in the future, lower the legs away from the body until they are 10-15 degrees from horizontal.

Advanced modification (legs 10-15 degrees from horizontal)

SHOULDER BRIDGE

Target area: *works spine mobility and strength, especially hip,*

buttock and hamstring muscles when raising and lowering.

1 Lie flat on back with legs bent, feet shoulder-width apart and arms by your side.

2 Breathing in, brace lower abdominal muscles whilst gently tilting pelvis backwards.

3 Breathing out, gently peel your lower back off the ground and roll your spine off the floor one vertebra at a time, raising your hips into the air until shoulders and knees are in a straight line.

4 Breathe in at the top of the movement and re-activate abdominal muscles to protect lower back.

5 Breathe out and lower the body in reverse motion, rolling the spine down to the floor with control back to the starting position.

SINGLE LEG STRETCH SEQUENCE

BENT-LEG

Target area: *works abdominal and leg muscles, whilst challenging the pelvis and neutral spine position.*

1 Lie flat on your back and raise legs to 90 degrees. Catch legs with both hands.

2 Activate neutral spine position and brace abdominal muscles.

3 Extend one leg out whilst the other leg is maintained at 90 degrees at hip and held gently with both hands. Aim to keep both feet at same height off the ground.

4 Keeping hips square, simultaneously straighten one leg whilst breathing out and bending the other catching the bent knee with your hands.

5 Perform the leg movement in a slow controlled motion whilst maintaining strong abdominal brace and deep breathing pattern.

6 Minimise any sideways movement of the legs by contracting the muscles of the legs at all times, pushing the leg out as though pushing the clutch peddle of a car.

7 Raise shoulders and head off the ground, to increase the intensity of the exercise on the abdominal muscles.

OBLIQUE TWIST

Target area: *works rectus abdominal, oblique and leg muscles.*

1 Having just completed the bent leg single leg stretch, stay in the same position with the legs and place the hands behind the head.

2 Keeping hips square, simultaneously straighten one leg whilst breathing out and bending the other bringing the opposite elbow towards the opposite knee.

3 Breathing in, twist the torso, taking the left elbow towards the right knee, whilst extending the left leg in a slow controlled motion.

4 Breathe out. Repeat movement with the right elbow to left knee.

5 Maintain a strong body position, avoiding sloppy or uneven movements whilst bending and straightening legs. Maintain a good rhythm.

PILATES PRINCIPLES LEG AND WAIST WORKOUT SUMMARY

EXERCISE	DESCRIPTION
1. Warm-up 1 Abdominal Bracing	Neutral spine and abdominal bracing.
2. Warm-up 2 Swimming	Lower back, neutral spine and co-ordination.
3. Lateral Leg Lifts	Leg and inner and outer thigh.
4. Ins and Outs	Leg and buttock.
5. The Hundred Drill	Abdominal.
6. Shoulder Bridge	Lower back.
7. Repeat – Lateral Leg Lifts (other leg) 8. Repeat – Ins and Outs (other leg)	
9. Single Leg Stretch bent leg	
10. Single Leg Stretch oblique twist	

NOTE: Go to stretching sequence to warm down.

YOGA STRETCHING PRINCIPLES 10 STRETCH BASICS

1. Lower Back	Lying on the floor, clasp your hands under your knees and gently pull your knees into your chest and hold. Raise head and shoulders off ground to increase stretch.
2. Hip and Buttock	Cross right foot over left knee. Clasp hands behind right thigh and gently pull the leg in towards you. Raise head and shoulders off ground to increase stretch. Switch legs.
3. Spinal Twist	Lying on the floor with your arms out to the side, place left foot on the right knee. Slowly lower legs to the left side whilst turning your head to the right. Switch sides.
4. Thigh Lie	Lie down on side. Bend your leg at the knee and grasp with hand. Pull heel into buttocks to stretch. Switch legs.
5. Lower Back and Abdominal Muscles	Lie on stomach and elbows. Brace stomach muscles and gently raise chest up, keeping arms bent, to stretch lower back and abdominal muscles.

6. Inner Thigh	Sit on floor with feet pressed together. Grip ankles with hands and place forearms along legs. Keeping abs in, push knees down towards floor with elbows until you feel a gentle stretch in your inner thighs.
7. Hip Flexor	Extend left leg forward and kneel on the right leg. Place hands on forward leg for support. Lower hip towards ground by increasing the angle whilst keeping the chest high and shoulders back. Switch legs.
8. Hip Reach	Continue position as above. Place left forearm across left knee and take right arm back overhead and to the side to stretch. Switch legs and arms.
9. Hamstrings	Bend right leg and rest on knee whilst straightening the left leg on heel. Keep toes back towards shin and place both hands above knee. Gently lean forward to stretch hamstrings. Switch legs.
10. Calves	On hands and toes, straighten your legs and rest one foot on top of the opposite heel. Gently press heel to the floor. Switch legs.

Hip, Butt and Thigh Muscle Toning Chair Exercises

Important points

• Gain your doctor's approval to perform these exercises, before starting.

• Start gently with 20 seconds and exercise within your own personal limits before progressing.

• Adapt 3Bs Exercise Principle™: Brace, Breath and Body Position with each exercise to ensure good technique and form.

• Stop if you feel discomfort, dizziness or pain. Seek appropriate medical advice before resuming.

• Use a solid stable chair on a flat, non-slip surface with a clear space around you. Place chair against a solid wall for added support.

WARM-UP DRILL AND STRETCH

STEP-UPS: 60 SECONDS

1 Stand tall with feet together, hands on hips, in front of a strong, stable chair (or 30cm high platform) placed against wall for support.

2 Place the left foot up on the chair and step up with the right foot to stand upright on the chair. Lower in reverse sequence and repeat by starting with opposite foot.

NOTE: Place chair against wall for support and balance.

STRETCH THIGHS AND HAMSTRINGS

THIGH

Stand tall, bend right leg behind body, grasp with hand and pull heel in towards buttocks. Repeat with left leg.

HAMSTRING

1 Take left leg forward and straighten, with toes pulled back towards shins and the other leg bent. Rest both hands above knee to support the lower back and gently lean forward.

2 Repeat with right leg.

RAISED LUNGES

1 Stand in extended forward lunge position with rear foot pointed and resting on solid stable chair, and forward knee aligned over foot.

2 With hands on hips for balance, breathe in as you lower your body, with the rear knee dropping to a soccer ball height from the ground for a beginner, or a tennis ball height from the ground for the more advanced.

3 Avoid your hip dropping to one side or body bending forward. Instead, keep your stomach muscles braced and body position strong by keeping chest high and torso long.

4 Breathe out as you raise the body up.

5 Complete exercise with one leg forward, then swap legs.

CALF RAISES

1 Stand tall, with feet close together and hands resting on back of chair.

2 Breathing out, raise heels up off the ground and balance on your toes, hold briefly, then lower keeping legs straight at all times.

WIDE SQUAT

1 Stand with feet approximately one to two shoulder-widths apart, knees over toes and hands resting forward on chair.

2 Breathing in, slowly bend your knees and sit back as you lower legs to right angles (90 degrees).

3 Breathe out as you straighten legs and return to the upright starting position.

4 Keep your knees aligned over your toes throughout the whole movement up and down, without rolling inwards.

NOTE: Lower only a short distance down if you are a beginner or haven't exercised in a while, until your muscles adapt.

LATERAL LEG RAISE

1 Stand tall, feet together, body sideways to solid stable chair, with one hand on hip and the closest hand supported with chair.

2 Bracing your stomach muscles, lean body slightly inwards to chair.

3 Breathing out, raise outer leg away from your body, out to the side, keeping heel as highest point.

4 Breathe in and lower leg.

5 Complete set then change sides.

HEEL PRESS

1 Stand tall in front of stable chair, with hands resting on backrest for support.

2 Bend one leg, lean body slightly forward and brace stomach muscles.

3 Move bent leg back slightly behind supporting leg as a starting point.

4 Breathing out, push heel of foot upwards without straightening leg, arching the lower back, twisting the hip or turning foot out to the side.

5 Complete set then change legs.

FORWARD LEG RAISE

1 Stand tall, feet together, body sideways to solid stable chair, with one hand on hip and the closest hand supported with chair.

2 Bracing your stomach muscles, become long throughout the body like a ballet dancer and point toes of one leg forward in front of you.

3 Breathing out, raise leg up until parallel to ground, without losing strong body position.

4 Breathe in and lower leg.

5 Complete set then change sides.

HAMSTRING BRIDGE

1 Lie on back, legs bent at 90 degrees with heels resting on strong stable chair, arms by your side.

2 Brace stomach muscles and breathe in.

3 Breathing out, raise pelvis off the ground and into the air to form a straight line between shoulder and knee driving through the buttocks and hamstring muscles.

4 Breathe in as you lower your body to the ground.

HAND SLIDE

1 To strengthen your waistline, lie on your back with knees bent and calves resting up on chair, arms extended forwards, hands resting on thighs.

2 Place small rolled up hand towel under the arch of lower back for support.

3 Breathing out, tense abdominal muscles, raise shoulders off ground and slide hands up towards knees.

4 Breathe in and lower, keeping stomach tense at all times until exercise completed.

CHEST CROSS-OVERS

1 Lie on your back with legs bent and raised on chair, arms crossed and resting on chest.

2 Breathe out, raise shoulders up and angle left shoulder across towards right knee.

3 Breathe in as you lower shoulders.

4 Repeat movement to the opposite side with right shoulder angling towards left knee.

HIP, BUTT AND THIGH MUSCLE CHAIR TONING SUMMARY

EXERCISE	DESCRIPTION		
Warm-up Step-ups	60 seconds.		
Stretch Thighs and Hamstrings	Stretch one leg, then the other. Hold each stretch for 15 seconds.		
1. Raised Lunges	Repeat both legs.		
2. Calf Raises	Utilise 20-30-40 Exercise Principle™.		
3. Wide Squat	Utilise 20-30-40 Exercise Principle™.		

4. Lateral Leg Raises	Repeat both legs. Keep heel as highest point.	
5. Heel Press	Repeat both legs.	
6. Forward Leg Raise	Repeat both legs.	
7. Hamstring Bridge	Utilise 20-30-40 Exercise Principle™.	
8. Hand Slide	Utilise 20-30-40 Exercise Principle™.	
9. Chest Cross-Overs	Utilise 20-30-40 Exercise Principle™.	

TRIMMER WAIST WORKOUT

WARM-UP DRILL AND STRETCH

SIDE SQUAT: 60 SECONDS

STRETCH THIGHS AND HAMSTRINGS

See page 30.

1 Stand tall with feet together and hands on hips.

2 Brace stomach muscles.

3 Breathe in and step to the left side into a wide squat position and lower – keeping knees over the line of the toes.

4 Breathe out and raise up, returning to the starting position.

5 Repeat movement across to the right side, then back to the left and so on, maintaining a strong abdominal brace.

ALTERNATE LEG LUNGES

Ensure your hips stay square and your knee remains over the line of
the toes at all times: up and down, without sideways movement.

1 Stand tall with feet together and hands on hips.

2 Brace stomach muscles.

3 Breathing in, lunge forwards with left leg, lowering rear knee towards the ground without touching the ground.

4 Keep body upright and chest high.

5 Breathing out, drive up and back through your legs to the upright standing position.

6 Repeat movement with right leg, then back to the left and so on.

HEEL PRESS

1 Kneel on all fours and brace stomach muscles.

2 Bend and raise one leg slightly off ground.

3 Breathing out, slowly push heel back and up towards ceiling without arching the lower back or twisting leg out to the side.

4 Breathe in and lower, maintaining a strong body position.

5 Complete set then change legs.

SIDE-LYING LEG LIFT

1 Lie on the left side of your body and brace stomach muscles.

2 Bend your left leg and straighten the right leg on top.

3 Breathing out, raise the right leg keeping your heel as the highest point.

4 Breathe in and lower.

5 Complete set then change sides.

HAND SLIDE

(SEE PHOTO ON PAGE 49)

1 To strengthen waistline, lie on your back with knees bent, arms extended forwards, hands resting on thighs.

2 Place small rolled up hand towel under the arch of the lower back for support (if necessary).

3 Breathing out, tense abdominal muscles, raise shoulders off ground and slide hands up towards knees.

4 Breathe in and lower, keeping stomach tense at all times until exercise completed.

HAMSTRING BRIDGE

1 Lie on back, legs bent at 90 degrees with heels resting on strong stable chair, arms by your side.

2 Brace stomach muscles and breathe in.

3 Breathing out, raise pelvis off the ground and into the air to form a straight line between shoulder and knee driving through buttocks and hamstring muscles.

4 Breathe in as you lower your body to the ground.

REVERSE CURLS

1 Lie on back with knees bent and arms down by your side.

2 Brace stomach muscles.

3 Keeping legs and stomach braced, breathe out and raise heels off ground bringing knees in towards chest.

4 Breathe out as you lower your legs.

5 Touch the ground without relaxing legs or stomach and repeat movement until set completed.

ELBOW-TO-KNEE

1 Lie on your back with your knees bent.

2 Bend your left leg and place it across your right knee.

3 Place your right hand behind your head and your left arm down by your side.

4 Brace stomach muscles.

5 Breathing out, raise your head and shoulders off the ground, your right elbow crossing towards your left knee.

6 Breathe in and lower back without relaxing your stomach.

7 Complete set and swap sides.

STRAIGHT-LEG SCISSORS

1 Lie on your back with legs straight, one leg lowered, the other vertical.

2 Depending on your flexibility, hold the back of your calf or hamstring muscles with your hands.

3 Brace stomach muscles.

4 Inhale.

5 Breathe out and in a scissor-like motion simultaneously raise one leg and lower the other catching the upper leg with both hands. Breathing may increase and intensify if leg speed increases.

6 Raise your shoulders and head off the ground to increase the intensity of the exercise on your stomach muscles, if your flexibility allows.

Avoid any sideways movement. Keep legs straight and aligned. Maintain a strong body position and keep stomach braced throughout the exercise.

TRIMMER WAISTLINE WORKOUT SUMMARY

EXERCISE	DESCRIPTION	
Warm-up Side Squat	60 seconds.	
Stretch Thighs and Hamstrings	Stretch one leg, then the other. Hold each stretch for 15 seconds.	
1. Alternate Leg Lunges	Alternate legs, one leg then straight to the other.	
2. Heel Press	Repeat both legs.	

3. Side-lying Leg Lifts	Repeat both legs.	
4. Hamstring Bridge	Utilise 20-30-40 Exercise Principle™.	
5. Hand Slide	Utilise 20-30-40 Exercise Principle™.	
6. Reverse Curls	Utilise 20-30-40 Exercise Principle™.	
7. Elbow-to-Knee	Repeat both sides.	
8.Straight-leg Scissors	Utilise 20-30-40 Exercise Principle™.	

PUTTING IT INTO PRACTICE

Making a commitment to regular exercise is an important part of achieving firmer thighs and a trimmer waist. Combining daily heart and lung (cardiovascular) fitness and muscle toning exercises with a healthy eating plan will help guide you towards your health goals. The World Health Organisation (WHO) recommends 30 minutes of moderate intensity physical activity every day for good health. To help put this plan into practice, I have devised a 3 Step Personal Training Plan as follows:

STEP 1: PLAN YOUR EXERCISE

Set aside time each day to exercise in the chart provided. Copy this chart and place it somewhere you can see it, for example, on your fridge door. Fill out the exercise carried out daily and weekly. Keep motivated by varying your exercise each week, or training with a friend.

WEEKLY EXERCISE CHART		
	Heart & Lung Fitness Example: walking, cycling, hiking, dancing, jogging etc.	Muscle Toning Exercise Example: Pilates Principles Leg and Waist Workout; Trimmer Waistline Workout; Yoga Stretching Basics
DAY	Record exercise and exercise time (minutes)	Record exercise and exercise time (minutes)
Monday		
Tuesday		
Wednesday		
Thursday		
Friday		
Saturday		
Sunday		
TOTAL WEEKLY EXERCISE TIME		

STEP 2: PLAN YOUR MEALS WITH THE 3 HOUR RULE® DAILY DIET PLANNER

Setting aside time each day to plan your meals is a highly successful way to help you tone up, lose weight, look good and feel great. Most diets recommend three meals and two snacks or five smaller meals a day, plus water. To put this into practice, I have designed the revolutionary 3 Hour Rule®, an eating system that helps you develop a healthy eating pattern for today's hectic modern society. In simple terms, to eat five smaller meals (or three meals and two snacks) a day, equates to eating approximately every three hours hence, the 3 Hour Rule®. It's that simple. By planning what and when you will eat, you can regulate your eating patterns, portion sizes, energy levels and your weight more effectively. In between meals aim to drink more water to fulfill your body's needs of eight glasses per day (more is needed with exercise).

3 HOUR RULE® TIME FRAME

The 3 Hour Rule® plays a vital role in developing a new eating routine based on consuming five smaller meals a day or three meals and two snacks. But this doesn't mean you are restricted to eating at exactly every three hours. Instead it offers flexibility by working within a range of 2.5-3.5 hours as shown in the table below. This time frame keeps you on track with five meals a day. It also helps you control the meal size or meal portion, teaching you how quickly foods digest. This means you can still eat foods you enjoy, but in a smaller amount so you are ready to eat again approximately three hours later. This keeps your metabolism high as well as your energy levels. It also helps you identify poor eating habits such as eating when stressed or drinking too much caffeine or soft drinks instead of eight glasses of water a day. If you miss a meal, don't worry – just get back on track as soon as possible. This is the flexibility offered with the 3 Hour Rule®.

	3 HOUR RULE®	TIME RANGE	
Meal 1 Breakfast	7am	7.00am	As the day progresses, so does the flexibility of the 3 Hour Rule®. The aim is to control your meal portions, focusing on five smaller* meals a day. If you miss a meal or make a mistake, simply get back on track as soon as possible. If you plan your meals this limits mistakes and allows you to develop a new eating routine. Carrying a water bottle will help curb any cravings and supply the essential fluids we all need between meals.
Meal 2 Snack	10am	Between 9.30 – 10.30am	
Meal 3 Lunch	1pm	Between 12.30 – 1.30pm	
Meal 4 Snack	4pm	Between 3.30 – 4.30pm	
Meal 5 Dinner	7pm	Between 6.30 – 7.30pm	

*In most cases 'smaller' refers to foods high in fibre and are filling but low in calories (ie. salads, bran cereal, vegetables, fruit).

2-DAY MEAL ROTATION™

It is very important to have a number of healthy meal choices available and to rotate them regularly so you can gain maximum nutritional value. The initial approach is based on adapting a 2-Day Meal Rotation™ of healthy food choices for breakfast, snacking, lunch and dinner just like a menu from a healthy café.

A 2-Day Meal Rotation™ involves not eating the same meal two days in a row. For example, if you eat breakfast cereal on Monday morning, eat baked beans on Tuesday morning, before repeating Monday's meal again. This way you begin to have a selection of meals to choose from that provide all the essential nutrients. You also feel more satisfied by having variety in your meals.

EXAMPLE OF 2-DAY MEAL ROTATION™ MEAL PLAN:

DAY 1	3 HOUR RULE®	MEAL DESCRIPTION
Meal 1 Breakfast	7am	One cup of cereal and milk; one piece of wholegrain toast with peanut spread; one glass of water.
Meal 2 Snack	10am (9.30-10.30am)	One tub of yogurt; one piece of fruit; one glass of water.
Meal 3 Lunch	1pm (12.30-1.30pm)	Lean meat (100g turkey) and salad sandwich on wholegrain bread; one glass of water.
Meal 4 Snack	4pm (3.30-4.30pm)	30 grams of mixed raw nuts; one glass of water.
Meal 5 Dinner	7pm (6.30-7.30pm)	Lean piece of red meat (120 grams) with 1–2 cups of mixed vegetables with one tablespoon of flaxseed oil; one glass water; 200g strawberry yogurt for dessert.

DAY 2	3 HOUR RULE®	MEAL DESCRIPTION
Meal 1 Breakfast	7am	One serve (220g can) of baked beans on two slices of wholegrain toast; one glass of water.
Meal 2 Snack	10am (9.30-10.30am)	One apple; one glass of water.
Meal 3 Lunch	1pm (12.30-1.30pm)	Fresh salad made with 100 grams of canned salmon; slice of cheese and tablespoon of olive oil; one glass of water.
Meal 4 Snack	4pm (3.30-4.30pm)	One tub yogurt; one glass of water.
Meal 5 Dinner	7pm (6.30-7.30pm)	One bowl of home-made chicken (100 grams) and vegetable soup; one wholemeal roll; one portion of low-fat ice-cream.

NOTE: Drink extra water throughout the day. Active people may need more meal portions to satisfy energy levels. Rotate meals regularly to gain all the essential nutrients required for good health.

GOOD FOOD LIST

A useful way of making better meal choices is to select natural foods instead of processed, refined, fast or fried foods. This is because many manufactured foods are high in saturated fats and sugars, which contribute to the excess energy that is a major cause of obesity. At the same time, one must also learn to enjoy a wide variety of nutritious foods in manageable portions. Only consuming one type of natural food choice can limit the intake of essential nutrients required by the body, which causes more harm than good.

So, instead of restricting foods, learn to balance them together in manageable portions. One of my goals as your personal coach is to educate you about healthy food choices that contain all the essential nutrients the body requires. In the food list that I have created you will not see many manufactured foods or drinks (apart from cereals, grains and dairy products) for the simple reason that the body does not require them.

This does not mean that foods not listed are forbidden. It simply means we can live without them, especially whilst aiming to lose weight. In time you must become aware of these 'non-essential' foods and drinks so you can make positive changes to your health. So, if you can't live without foods such as chocolate or drinks such as coffee or alcohol, don't try to. Start by halving the quantity you normally have, and focus on developing a new eating routine with the assistance of the 3 Hour Rule® and 2-Day Meal Rotation™.

GOOD PROTEIN SOURCES

PROTEIN FROM ANIMAL SOURCES

LEAN MEATS

Aim to eat 1-2 portions (100-200 grams) of animal-based protein a day. It is important to choose lean meat protein sources low in saturated fat. You can do this by: choosing lean red meats; trimming fat from meat and skin from poultry before cooking; not frying or roasting in fat or oil. Instead, use low fat cooking methods such as stir frying and grilling. In these ways, you can reduce the overall fat and saturated fat content of your diet.

• **Organic beef, pork or lamb are best.**

POULTRY

• **Organic or free-range chicken**
• **turkey.**

FISH AND SHELLFISH

• **All fresh forms: steamed, grilled, poached, barbecued**
• **canned forms: tuna, salmon, mackerel, sardines.**

NOTE: Avoid eating battered, commercially packaged or deep fried fish or shellfish.

EGGS

• **Poached, boiled, scrambled and omelettes prepared healthily, ie. boiled, poached or cooked in minimal oil.**

PROTEIN FROM PLANT SOURCES

Aim to eat one portion per day, or at least every second day.

NUTS AND SEEDS

• **30 grams ($^1/_2$ palmful) of mixed raw nuts and seeds: raw or blanched almonds and cashews; sesame or pepita seeds**
• **one teaspoon of peanut or almond spread.**

BEANS AND PEAS (LEGUMES)

• **One cup of cooked: kidney beans, split peas, chick peas, lentils, canned (baked) beans, dried beans or $^1/_2$ cup of low-fat hummus.**

SOY

• **One cup of cooked soy beans**
• **100 grams of tofu or tempeh.**

GOOD PROTEIN SOURCES

(continued)

PROTEIN FROM CALCIUM SOURCES

Aim to eat two portions a day. Choose low-fat variations, wherever possible.

- **One cup (250ml) of reduced fat milk or calcium fortified soy milk**

- **200 grams of low-fat yogurt**

- **200 grams of natural fruit yogurt with friendly bacteria (ABC)**

- **150ml yogurt drink**

- **20-40 grams of low-fat cheese**

- **50-100 grams of low-fat cottage, fetta or ricotta cheese.**

GOOD CARBOHYDRATE SOURCES

FRESH VEGETABLES AND SALADS

Consume around two cups per day of cooked vegetables or three cups of loosely packed salad.

- **Green leafy vegetables and sprouts are best, including: celery, lettuce, spinach, silver beet, asparagus, cauliflower, broccoli, snow peas, capsicum, Brussels sprouts, bean sprouts, watercress, cabbage, bok choy**
- **Also: avocado, potato, parsnip, pumpkin, sweet potato, green beans, cucumber, tomato, carrots, leeks, lentils, yellow squash, beetroot, eggplant, radishes, zucchini, corn, mushrooms, turnips, onions, spring onions, garlic.**

GRAINS

- **1/3 cup of muesli**
- **one cup of wholegrain breakfast cereal (low sugar and salt)**
- **one cup of rolled oats (porridge)**
- **one cup of cooked basmati or jasmine rice**
- **one cup of cooked brown rice**
- **one cup cooked wholemeal pasta**
- **one cup of barley**
- **one cup millet**
- **one cup buckwheat.**

WHOLEGRAIN BREADS

- **One slice wholegrain bread**
- **one slice of yeast-free bread**
- **$^1/_2$ English muffin**
- **$^1/_2$ pita bread**
- **one small wholegrain roll**
- **one corn tortilla.**

Fresh Fruits

Aim to eat 1–2 portions a day. Remember: fresh is best!

- **Apples, apricots, blackberries, pears, cherries, grapes, paw-paw, peaches, lychees, raspberries, strawberries**
- **bananas, dates, figs, prunes, raisins, dried fruits**
- **grapefruits, limes, kiwi fruits, oranges, lemons, pineapples, mandarins, tomatoes, passionfruits**
- **cantaloupe (rockmelon), watermelon, honeydew melon, other melons.**

NOTE: fruit juice should be limited to 125ml or ½ cup at any one time due to its concentrated source of sugar which counts as one portion.

Essential Fat Sources

- **Omega 3s found in fish, nuts, seeds, flaxseed, linseed and olive oils (one teaspoon per day)**
- **avocado is great when added to salads or sandwiches!**

Drinks

- **Water is best: try to drink eight glasses of filtered or spring water per day**
- **vegetable juice: such as fresh carrot or celery juice**
- **smoothies: ice, skim milk, fruit**
- **acidophilus drinking yogurt**
- **herb and green tea (in moderation).**

AVOID: Alcohol, coffee, black tea, soft drinks, fruit juices and cordials. Drink as occasional treat only.

SUMMARY OF GOOD FOOD LIST

FOOD GROUP	MEAL PORTIONS
1. COMPLEX CARBOHYDRATES (FIBRE)	
• **Cereals and Grains**	• **Four portions a day. Active people may need more.**
• **Vegetables and Salads**	• **Four portions a day. Active people may need more.**
• **Fruits**	• **1-2 portions a day.**
2. PROTEIN	
• **Protein (A) Animal Source**	• **1-2 lean portions a day (100-200 grams).**
• **Protein (P) Plant Source**	• **One portion per day, or at least every second day.**
• **Protein (C) Calcium Source**	• **Two portions a day.**
3. DIETARY FATS	
• **Olive or flaxseed oil***	• **One tablespoon may be used on salads or across cooked vegetables.**
4. WATER	• **6-8 glasses per day. More if actively exercising.**

* Generally no extra dietary fats are needed if consuming recommended daily protein and carbohydrate portions. If anything, you need to monitor the unseen dietary fats in foods from the way they are cooked, prepared or packaged.

STEP THREE: MAINTAINING MOTIVATION

With fitness programs it helps to have a personal target to achieve in a set period of time, with realistic expectations in mind. Use the information below to set personal goals.

- $^1/_2$ **kilogram (500 grams) weight loss per week is seen as a safe weight loss goal by the medical society.**

- **A 5% weight loss target is a realistic short-term goal over 12 weeks. For example, from 80 to 76 kilograms.**

- **Reducing your waistline to below 90cm for men and below 80cm for women.**

- **Being able to exercise longer without feeling tired. For example, progressing from 20 to 30 seconds with the 20-30-40 Exercise Principle™.**

- **Establishing periods throughout the year to look good for, such as: birthdays, weddings, functions, charity balls, Christmas and even trips away or activities such as skiing or trekking holidays.**

WHERE TO FROM HERE?

Knowing where you stand today, and working towards some (or all) of these goals on the previous page, will provide inspiration and motivation for you to pursue your goal of firmer thighs and a trimmer waist. The ingredients provided in this book help provide the framework for you to follow in order to achieve success. Remember, any small improvement in the future is a success, and you should be proud. Soon, you should begin to look better and feel better about your body. Also, there are little things to look forward to, such as being able to carry groceries without getting tired, or having more energy for longer periods throughout the day.

Think of it as being like putting the pieces of a 1000-piece jigsaw puzzle together. Some people may already have 500 pieces down before starting this program, while others may be starting from the beginning. Everyone is unique and will respond differently. The effort is up to you but I'm here to help you along the way! To look out for my next series of books, visit www.thebodycoach.com.

ABOUT THE AUTHOR

PAUL COLLINS, the Body Coach®, is an award-winning Personal Trainer who has helped thousands of men, women and children get fit, lose weight, look good and feel great.

Dubbed the 'fitness guru' by Inside Sport magazine and 'the trainers' trainer' by his fellow peers, Paul communicates his revolutionary coaching techniques through published work in magazines, newspapers and books, videos, making radio and television appearances and personal training.

A vocal advocate of the importance of personal health and physical conditioning, Paul has trained television stars and sporting champions including members of the Australian Swimming Team. He is a highly sought after corporate 'health and well-being' speaker represented by Saxton Speakers Bureau, Australia.

As a leader in the field of fitness, exercise and weight loss, Paul has successfully combined an elite sports background with a teaching degree in Personal Development, Health and Physical Education (PDHPE) along with international certification as a Strength and Conditioning Coach and Personal Trainer.

Paul is the creator of the revolutionary 3 Hour Rule® Diet System™ and the men's weight loss book *The Body Coach® How to Lose Your Love Handles*. Paul's products and seminars aim to revolutionise exercise and weight loss, motivating people to be fit and live an active, healthy lifestyle.

To learn more about Paul's books, educational products, seminars and personal training, visit: www.thebodycoach.com.